Da*ywalkS
Vale of Llangollen

a network of 27 linked footpath routes between
Chirk and the Horseshoe Falls exploring
the valley of the River Dee and the hills

by Gordon Emery & John Roberts

****
WALKWAYS
J S Roberts
8 Hillside Close, Bartley Green
Birmingham B32 4LT
****

DaywalkS: Vale of Llangollen
by Gordon Emery & John Roberts

Photo: Llantisilio Church (C) Storm Photography

ISBN 0 947708 26 X

First Published 1991

WALKWAYS

DaywalkS Footpath Networks

This series now includes networks of walks in
Arden
Cannock Chase
Chaddesley Woods
Clent & Lickey Hills
Elan Valley
Wyre Forest
Bridgnorth - Kinver - Stourport
with more planned.

All but the last two are currently in folded A2
sheet format, sold in a plastic cover. They will
gradually be replaced by expanded networks covering
the same areas in book form, like this one.

Long Distance Routes

Full step by step guides for walking in either
direction with sketch maps. You can start at a
number of midway points and these routes often
connect with each other and other Long Distance
Footpaths. (All are folded A2 sheets folded to
A5, but Heart of England Way is a book.)

Llangollen to Bala
Bala to Snowdon
Birmingham to Ludlow
Ludlow to Rhayader
Rhayader to Aberystwyth
Birmingham to Church Stretton
Heart of England Way

8 Hillside Close, Bartley Green, Birmingham B32 4LT
(Send sae for current list & prices.)

To enjoy the best of the countryside

Join The Ramblers.
 Explore the many hundreds of thousands of miles of Britain's beautiful footpaths and receive our exclusive Yearbook full of information on walking and places to stay.
 Plus regular colour magazines and newsletters — free of charge.
 You will also be entitled to valuable discounts at outdoor equipment shops.

And at the same time you will be helping us to protect the countryside and to look after Britain's footpaths

For further information and an application form, drop a line to:
The Ramblers' Association, 1-5 Wandsworth Road, London SW8 2X
Tel: 071-582 6878 (ii)

WALKS IN CLWYD ›

EXPLORE THE VILLAGES, MOUNTAINS, WOODS AND WATERWAYS OF CLWYD WITH THESE INFORMATIVE GUIDES.

EACH BOOKLET CONTAINS AN INTERESTING WALK — SHORTCUTS ARE INCLUDED — WITH DIRECTIONS, A MAP AND LINE DRAWINGS OF BUILDINGS, PLANTS AND ANIMALS.

26 DIFFERENT WALKING GUIDES AVAILABLE FROM BOOKSHOPS, TOURIST INFORMATION OFFICES AND CLWYD LIBRARIES. MOST STARTING POINTS ARE ON BUS ROUTES. **90p EACH**

Enquiries 0244 377955

The Authors

GORDON EMERY has been an apprentice printer, trainee glassblower, solicitor's clerk, road sweeper, truck driver, storeman, motorbike and car stunt show organiser, walk leader, barman, supervisor of a Community Project team, and has restored a Welsh cottage.

He became a walks writer when he helped produce 15 "Walks Around Wrexham Maelor" for Clwyd County Council and went on to write some 25 more and become his own publisher with "Walks in Clwyd". His latest is "Guide to the Maelor Way", a 24 mile trail from Whitchurch to Chirk.

Gordon is a Ramblers Association Footpath Inspector and has installed over 170 stiles and bridges. He lives in Chester with his wife, who is a violin and Alexander Technique teacher, and his two sons.

JOHN ROBERTS is much more boring because he was in insurance and served time as a Loss Adjuster. (Send sae for dull explanation). Then he gave up work to become a college lecturer and taught law and insurance.

He took up walking along Midland canals, finished them all and went on to footpaths. He joined the Ramblers Association and became editor of the Midland (and later Warwicks) Area newsletter.

John became a walks writer and self publisher after a vision on the road to Scarborough (the Cleveland Way) which gave him the insane idea of producing a Long Distance Footpath from Birmingham to Aberystwyth (I ask you), followed by Llangollen to

Snowdon. You can read the WALKWAYS list on page (i). For a change, he turned to Short Distance Footpaths in the form of the DaywalkS series, and he publishes the Heart of England Way guide.

Gordon worked out the basic plan for these walks and wrote the historical notes and other comments. He also discovered and punctuated Mr G H Steele's account of his visit to the area in 1818, which we quote verbatim. John wrote the purply descriptive bits about the landscape and did the detailed directions and maps. And they argued about the rest.

We thought you would prefer this to pictures of Gordon and John.

Pillar of Eliseg – page 63

Contents

Horseshoe Falls in the River Dee - page 66

The Landscape, some People & Places

The Vale of Llangollen is one of the beautiful
valleys of the River Dee (Afon Dyfyrdwy). After
making its way from the slopes of Dduallt (black
hillside) in the Snowdonia National Park it runs
down to Llyn Tegid (Bala Lake). In legend its
pure waters do not mix with those of the lake.

Leaving Bala, the Dee makes a horseshoe bend above
Berwyn to enter the Vale (of Llangollen). After
tumbling under the famous bridge in the centre of
Llangollen town, the river runs through green
meadows to Froncysyllte, effectively the eastern
gateway to the Vale. Then the Dee changes again
and starts a series of big loops as it curls away
onto the Cheshire plain.

The north side of the Vale is an escarpment, the
southern rampart of the great bulk of Ruabon
Mountain. This becomes a vast wall of white rock
as you move west and north. The mountain top is
brown moorland, familiar enough in Wales, but
limestone is not common and adds an unusual
prettiness a little like the Yorkshire Dales. You
notice this especially in the type of stone walls
and the limestone loving flora.

This escarpment reaches from the mouth of the Vale
to Llangollen, then curves north to form a
vertical wall to the enclosed upland valley of the
Eglwyseg River. Here Cistercian monks built Valle
Crucis Abbey in the early 13th century. The Offa's
Dyke Path now runs through the area beside these
exciting crags as it passes above Llangollen.

The southern side of the Vale is just as steep but
has a different geological structure so that only
shale and slate are in evidence. It is rather more
wooded, but again, dramatically beautiful.

(1)

The Vale was created by the glaciation of what is now the River Dee, although at that time it flowed south into what is now the River Severn. The Eglwyseg escarpment is composed of Carboniferous Limestone and to the east of it, beyond a clear fault distinguished by a ravine, the main mass of Ruabon Mountain consists of Cefn y Fedw Sandstone. You can see that the grass slopes over the limestone give way to gorse on the sandstone.

The steepling hill known as Dinas Bran, with the ruins of its eerie castle spying on the town, is neither sandstone nor limestone, but an inlier of of shale related to the Berwyn Mountains at the south of the Vale.

Few small areas have so many cultural and historical associations as this - Valle Crucis Abbey, Chirk Castle, the Ladies of Llangollen, the Llangollen Canal and Pontcysyllte Aqueduct, Castell Dinas Bran, a Motor Museum, a restored steam railway, Eliseg's Pillar and the International Eisteddfod.

People have visited and described the Vale of Llangollen for centuries. In 1854 George Borrow used Llangollen as a base for many expeditions, culminating in his two long walks across Wales which form the basis of "Wild Wales".

In 1818 a Mr G H Steele took a three week tour of Lancashire, Cheshire and North Wales. His handwritten account has, to our knowledge, never been put in print before, perhaps because no one has ever seen it, or perhaps because the original text had no punctuation whatsoever in the whole book. Gordon found it on the locked shelves of Chester Reference Library and we transcribe it here for the interested reader.

Mr Steele visited Froncysyllte to see Telford's aqueduct, he stayed in Llangollen, saw Valle Crucis Abbey, climbed Dinas Bran, saw the Eliseg Pillar and met the Ladies of Llangollen at their home, Plas Newydd. We have therefore let him describe these places and his words appear at suitable points, with Gordon's punctuation added. Spellings are unchanged from his original. This little book may be Mr Steele's only contribution to history, for Gordon could find no further mention of him anywhere.

These walks explore the limestone crags to the north, the little wooded hills and the pastures, and they visit the famous places. We have tried to say a little about most of them, but for more informative leaflets and books, visit the Tourist Information Centre in Llangollen.

Near Trevor Rocks on Route 24

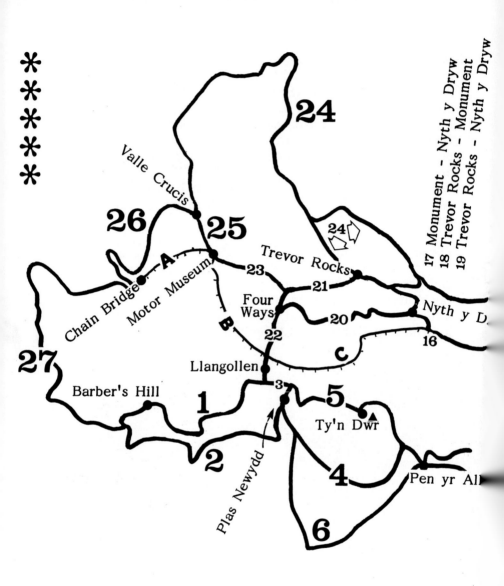

** ** ** **

24

Valle Crucis

26 25

17 Monument – Nyth y Dryw
18 Trevor Rocks – Monument
19 Trevor Rocks – Nyth y Dryw

24

Trevor Rocks

A
Chain Bridge Motor Museum 23
21
Four
Ways 20
B Nyth y D.
27 22 16
c
Llangollen
Barber's Hill 3 5
1 Ty'n Dwr
2 4 Pen yr All
Plas Newydd
6

Daywalk*S
Vale of Llangollen

Notes

(1) YHA Ty'n Dwr. See Route 5 for notes about starting from there.

(2) Route 24 from Valle Crucis forks to either Trevor Rocks or Monument.

(3) Castell Dinas Bran is on Route 21.

(4) For canal sections see page 67.

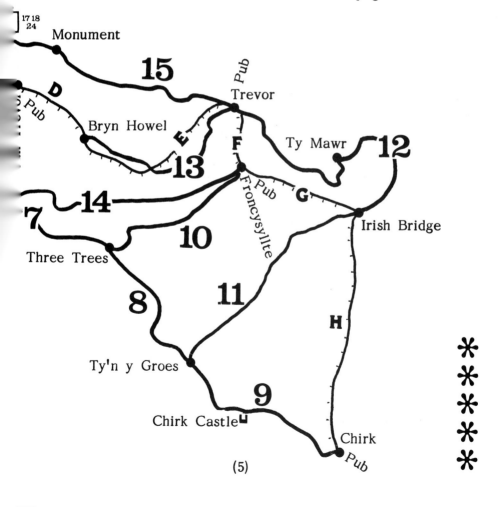

(5)

Using Daywalks

Once you have decided from the General Map on pages (4) & (5) which routes you want to walk:

* Decide where you want to start and look it up in the list of Junction and Starting Points; use your OS maps to get there.

* Jot down a list of your chosen routes in order. The paragraphs of directions are numbered in one direction and lettered in another, eg 4(1) is starting from Plas Newydd and 4(a) from Pen yr Allt, so include the letter or number of the first one. Slip your note in the plastic cover of the book.

Each route description ends with a note of the routes available from that point, with paragraph letters or numbers.

Publisher's Note
Amendment Service

The countryside changes all the time. You will meet new tracks, stiles, gates and barns; hedges vanish, paths are diverted and trees fall down. To keep directions up to date I issue amendment slips.

IF you write to tell me of any changes or problems that you meet, stating route and paragraph number, I will refund your postage.

IF you send me a stamped addressed envelope with a note of what publication(s) you have, I will send you up to date amendment slips.

John Roberts

Information & Transport

Buses: Chester - Wrexham - Trevor - Sun Trevor
— Llangollen - Bala - Barmouth

Trains: Chester - Wrexham - Ruabon - Chirk -
— Shrewsbury

The railway once ran down the Vale of Llangollen to
Bala. There is nothing left now but a few miles of
track restored by the Llangollen Railway Society
from Llangollen to Deeside Halt, which may reach
Glyndyfyrdwy by 1992. You could use this daytime
summer only service as a link in your walks.

For timetable information ask Llangollen Railway
Society (0978 860951 24hrs - 0978 860950 daytime),
British Rail (021 643 2711) or the Tourist
Information Office (0978 860828)

There is abundant accommodation and dozens of
places to eat and drink. Many of them are open the
year round. Contact the Tourist Information Office.

As once said, the only way to explore India was by
ox cart, and the only way to explore the Vale is
by Shank's Pony. However, for those who find it
easier to travel by car to reach the start of a
walk, there is a good network of minor roads. There
is a full list of Junction & Starting Points on
page (11) and we point out whether parking space is
available at each. In some cases you will be using
grass verges or other odd spots, if so park with
great care;

> USE a car park wherever possible
> NEVER obstruct narrow lanes
> ASSUME that field gates WILL be used.

You will need

* A MAP
There is a sketch map of each route in this book.
Normally we would suggest that you carry an
Ordnance Survey Landranger map for interest and to
help find starting points. The numbers of the
relevant sheets are below, but you would need
three. For these routes you can manage with a
general map such as a road atlas. Landranger
(1.25ins:1mile) sheets - 117 Chester, 125 Bala &
Lake Vyrnwy and 126 Shrewsbury. The Pathfinder
(2.5ins: -1mile) sheets are SJ 24/34 Llangollen &
Wrexham South, SJ 04/14 Corwen and SJ23/33 Chirk.

* CLOTHING & GEAR
Your own experience is the best guide in the long
run but if you have none, consider these points,
which are repeated from previous Daywalks guides:

(1) Boots. Most people seems to prefer them at
most times of year; go for the lightest that
you can find. Trainers are excellent in dry
weather and make progress so much easier.

(2) Socks. You don't necessarily need two pairs,
but a good thickness of woolly padding is a
great comfort. The traditional grey rough wool
"rag sock" is hardwearing and reasonably thick,
but that is about all. Try loop pile socks.

(3) Gaiters can keep you comfortable through
mud, flood and undergrowth and you can keep them
on in all but the hottest weather.

(4) Avoid jeans because they are cut too close
for comfortable walking. Denim may be fine in
California where it was first used by a Mr Levi

to make working trousers, but here it is hot in summer, cold in winter, holds the damp and is in any case heavy and stiff. In summer try polycotton trousers which are light and dry in no time. In colder weather corduroy is not bad. (In fact, Gordon disagrees with John's views on jeans, he likes them. Which shows one of the problems of writing a book jointly.)

(5) Take a waterproof, preferably hooded and long enough to reach down to your gaiters.

(6) Take a hat and gloves and something to keep out the wind such as a showerproof jacket. Your waterproof would do but they can be sweaty and uncomfortable. Many people speak well of wax jackets in this respect. Always carry an extra sweater.

(7) Good in all seasons is a long sleeved brushed cotton shirt which opens all down the front. You can wear it open or buttoned to various degrees, or not at all, with sleeves rolled up or down, inside or outside your trousers, to give ventilation or protection from sun, wind, vegetation and insects, as required.

This is general advice based mainly on ordinary clothing. Visit a good outdoor equipment shop and see if they have anything to offer which would improve your comfort. For example, windproof garments and magic vests which do not stay wet like cotton T shirts. First though, try ordinary clothes to find out whether and how they could be improved upon.

In many walking books you would be recommended to carry a compass, but it really is not necessary on any of these routes.

Rights of Way & Obstructions

DaywalkS routes are on public rights of way or well established paths and tracks. They may be Foot -paths, Bridleways or Byways (usually green lanes or tracks) with some stretches of ordinary road. Your rights as pedestrian are the same on all, you are entitled to follow the track or cross the land. The fact that it is "private" land (most land is) is quite irrelevant.

Occupiers of land are legally obliged not to obstruct paths, it is an offence, but sometimes they do. Paths should not be ploughed up nor have crops growing over them, nor should you meet barbed wire fences. You are entitled to cross or remove any such obstacles doing as little damage as you reasonably can. You may diverge to pass the obstacle so long as you go no further than is necessary and do not enter someone else's land.

We do not want to give the impression that most paths are blocked solid, they are not. But in a day's walking you may meet a couple of obstacles. There were no problems on these routes at the time of writing. If you meet any please write to the publisher so they can be referred to the County Council for attention.

The Ramblers' Association and other more local footpath and amenity groups have an important role in keeping footpaths open. The RA has Footpath Secretaries for each area who monitor the state of paths, respond to closure and diversion proposals and organise maintenance. If you use footpaths it seems right that you should support them. See their advert on page (ii).

Junctions & Starting Points

The places are listed alphabetically to help you find the start of your walk. You should not need this list again. The names are taken from the nearest place to the junction, but that may be at some distance. In a village the junction point may not be at the centre.

Some Junction Points are the corners of fields or tops of hills and only accessible on foot. You can't start there but they are places from which you have a choice of routes.

Each Starting Point is described so you will know it when you arrive, and a six digit map reference is given so you can find it on a map and use the roads to get there. (Map references are not absolutely precise and may be a hundred yards or so out, hence the extra description.) The OS maps show you how to use them.

Barber's Hill (SJ 199416) corner of lane where two tracks lead off; no parking.

Bryn Howel (SJ 249417) canal bridge below hotel; very limited parking.

Chain Bridge (SJ 199416) hotel on canal; car park & picnic place across lane to NW.

Chirk (SJ 284377) railway station; car park in village, pubs etc.

Four Ways (SJ 216428) three tracks and a lane meet; very limited parking.

Froncysyllte (SJ 271413) Aqueduct Inn on A5; parking in the area.

Irish Bridge (SJ 286407) canal bridge on A483; limited parking.

Llangollen (SJ 215421) Tourist Information Office on S side of Dee bridge; car parks in town.

Monument (SJ 245428) stile onto Panorama road at top edge of wood; limited parking.

Motor Museum (SJ 206435) canal towpath above entrance; car parking for patrons.

Nyth y Dryw (SJ 234417) corner of lane by gate; no parking.

Pen yr Allt (SJ 237410) grass track meets stone track by power pole; no road access.

Plas Newydd (SJ 217416) main entrance; car park.

Sun Trevor (SJ 241424) canal bridge below pub; limited parking.

Three Trees (SJ 252403) green field track meets T junction of lanes by three road signs; no parking.

Trevor Basin (SJ 271422) canal basin; pub, car park.

Trevor Rocks (SJ 433222) cattle grid where lane meets Panorama road; limited parking on road.

Ty'n Dwr (SJ 230414) youth hostel entrance; no parking.

Ty'n y Groes (SJ 263389) cottages on corner of lane with gate at end of track; very limited parking.

Ty Mawr (SJ 283415) Country Park; car park.

Valle Crucis Abbey (SJ 204442) lane to Abbey meets A542; very limited parking.

List of Routes

All routes are described in both directions, so Route (1) might have been called "Barber's Hill - Llangollen".

Some directions are repeated, for example, Routes 17,18 and 19 share the same path at Trevor Rocks. This should not cause any confusion but we mention it in case it seems odd. Occasionally you will see a mysterious and apparently useless piece of information, such as "ROUTE 6 RUNS L HERE." The rule is, if you don't want to know, ignore it. However you might want to know if, say, you had taken Route 1 to Llangollen and intended then to use Route 5 without going to the middle of town. It is just to help you when part of a route is shared.

You can walk the towpath of the Llangollen Canal which is shown by dotted lines on the maps as routes (A) to (H). They are not described in detail since a canal is a canal and there are no branches, but we do tell you what to look for when you arrive at a Junction Point.

	Route	Miles	Kms
1	Llangollen - Barber's Hill	2.6	4.2
2	Barber's Hill - Plas Newydd	2.5	4
3	Llangollen - Plas Newydd	.6	1
4	Plas Newydd - Pen yr Allt	2.8	3
5	Llangollen - Pen yr Allt	1.8	1.3
6	Plas Newydd - Pen yr Allt	2.7	4.5
7	Pen yr Allt - Three Trees	1.3	2
8	Ty'n y Groes - Three Trees	1.3	2
9	Chirk - Ty'n y Groes	1.8	3
10	Froncysyllte - Three Trees	1.8	3

(13)

		Miles	Kms
11	Ty'n y Groes - Irish Bridge	2.2	3.5
12	Irish Bridge - Trevor Basin	2.7	4.3
13	Trevor Basin - Bryn Howel	1.7	2.8
14	Froncysllte - Pen yr Allt	2.5	4
15	Trevor Basin - Monument	1.8	3
16	Nyth y Dryw - Sun Trevor	.6	1
17	Monument - Nyth y Dryw	1.4	2.3
18	Trevor Rocks - Monument	1.6	2.5
19	Trevor Rocks - Nyth y Dryw	.6	1
20	Four Ways - Nyth y Dryw	1.3	2
21	Four Ways - Trevor Rocks	.9	1.5
22	Llangollen - Four Ways	.4	.7
23	Four Ways - Motor Museum	.9	1.5
24	Valle Crucis - Trevor Rocks	4.2	7
	or Monument	5.5	9
25	Motor Museum - Valle Crucis	.6	1
26	Chain Bridge - Valle Crucis	1.5	2.5
27	Chain Bridge - Barbers Hill	3.3	5.3

Llangollen Canal Sections

		Miles	Kms
(A)	Chain Bridge - Motor Museum	.6	1
(B)	Motor Museum - Llangollen	1.3	2
(C)	Llangollen - Sun Trevor	1.8	3
(D)	Sun Trevor - Bryn Howel	.6	1
(E)	Bryn Howel - Trevor Basin	1.6	2.6
(F)	Trevor Basin - Froncysllte	.6	1
(G)	Froncysllte - Irish Bridge	1.3	2
(H)	Irish Bridge - Chirk	2.6	4.3

Sample Circuits

Start	Routes	Miles	Kms
Llangollen	22-21-19-16-C	4.4	7.1
Trevor Basin	12-11-8-10-F	8.5	13.7
Plas Newydd	5-14-F-15-18-21-22-3	10.4	16.7
Chirk	Outer Circle	30.3	48.8

Main Map Symbols

Starting point	●
Path	⋯⋯
Track	– – – –
Road/lane	⤙
Hedge/fence/wall	⊥
Railway	┼┼┼┼┼┼
Canal	⁓
Stream	⁓
Rivers, lakes & ponds	⁓
Church	+
Building	■
Car park	◻
Edge of woodland	⁓

Map scale appx 1.5 ins:mile 2.3 cms:km

1 Llangollen - Barber's Hill
2.8 miles 4.5 kms

This route lifts you from the town on a steep track
through a wood, up and up until you come out of
the trees onto the hills. The whole splendid
panorama of the Vale is around you, with
Llangollen far below.

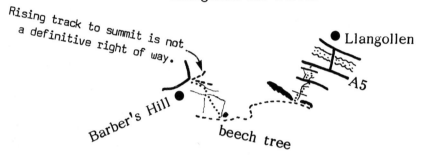

Mr Steele arrives in Llangollen .....

" We then proceeded in the Chaise to Llangollen, a
distance of 4 or 5 miles. This town lies in a most
delightful Vally, the Scenery delightfully
Picturesque. For two miles before you enter this
Town the Prospect is almost enchanting: upon one
side runs the River Dee - surrounded by Mountains
of various heights. On the other side, above you,
the Canal. Upon your right are some immense Rocks.

" Upon our entrance into the Town of Llangollen we
cross the Dee over a neat stone Bridge; arrived
about 2 o'clock. We put up our chaise at the King's
Head [now the Royal Hotel], being the first House
we came to over the Bridge upon the left-hand. We
met with a Musical Reception at this place for on
our entrance observed an Old Welsh Harper who
performed the whole time. He remained there after
seeing our House taking care of given orders for
our Dinner."

(16)

✳

Llangollen to Barber's Hill

(1) Leaving Tourist Information Office go R to T junction at A5

(2) Go R, pass Post Office & on 100 yds to take path L (opposite West St).

(3) Cross road & enter cul de sac ahead (ignore track R). Take path up R before end house (Craig View), to top of bank.

(4) Go L with railings & join path between railings, to lane.

(5) Cross, take stile, go R up hedges via stiles to wood.

(6) Go L to join track, then up R. Pass L bend & ruin, then R bend. Pass track R & on 100 yds to end of wall R by beech.

(7) Cross gate/stile R (may be bust) then over wire fence to open field.

(8) Note field boundaries & cross diagonally over crest to opposite corner. Cross fence to field L, then stile.

(9) Path may be hidden by bracken. Go L to hawthorn then down path to wall. Go L to stile, tracks & road bend.

Barber's Hill
●
>> OPTIONS <<
Routes 2(1) & 27 (a)

Barber's Hill to Llangollen

(a) From where tracks meet road bend, take stile. Go L up wall to 3rd tree.

(b) Take path up R thro bracken to hawthorn. Pass it on your R & keep same line to take stile.

(c) Go L & cross fence. NB field edges & cross diagonally over crest to far corner. Cross gate/stile (?bust) to track.

(d) Go L appx .7 mile, past ruin & down steeply. As slope eases walk on L side, watch for signpost & stile below L. (If you meet waterworks R you are 10 yds over.)

(e) Take stile & follow hedges for 3 fields via stiles, to lane.

(f) Take path opposite. Fork R with railings, then R down path behind house to entry.

(e) Cross road & on to A5, go R to traffic lights.

(f) Go L to Tourist Information Centre.

Llangollen
●
>> OPTIONS <<
Routes 3(1), 5(1), 22(1), (B) or (C)

(17)

2

Barber's Hill - Plas Newydd
2.5 miles   4 kms

This route uses one of the many narrow, winding lanes leading up from the town into the hills. It is an easy alternative to the breathtakingly steep Route 1, and the views are nearly as good.

Plas Newydd, former home of the "Ladies of Llangollen" is open to the public in summer. The colourful and immaculate gardens are open all year. See Mr G H Steele's account of the ladies, the house and the gardens.

Plas Newydd

Plas Newydd

Barber's Hill

beech tree

Barber's Hill to Plas Newydd

(1) At road bend & tracks, put your back to tracks & go L appx 300 yds & take stile L.

(2) Go diagonally upfield & cross shoulder of hill to stile & lane.

(3) Go L & take first track L appx .6 mile. Watch for start of wall L at big beech & go appx 100 yds to track junction.

(4) Take track R to iron barn, then gate R to pass barn on your L.

(5) Follow green track with fence on your R & take gate (?bust) into wood. On to lane.

(6) Go L appx 1 mile, passing lane L, to lane junction at entrance of

Plas Newydd.
●

>> OPTIONS <<
Routes 3(a), 4(1) & 6(1)

Plas Newydd to Barber's Hill

(a) Put your back to Plas Newydd entrance & go half L up Grange Rd. Follow appx 1 mile via;

- sharp R bend
- past lane R
- past path R
- past farms (1), (2) & (3)

Go on 200 yds & take gate R to iron fenced path.

(b) Go up thro wood & exit via gate (?bust), then green track past iron barn & take gate. Go L up field edge to track.

(c) Go L to lane. Go R, round R bend to next bend corner & take stile R.

(d) Go ahead, bearing R over shoulder of hill & take bottom corner stile to lane. Go R 300 yds to corner with 2 tracks off.

Barber's Hill
●

(Rising track leads to summit and radio mast. Not a definitive right of way.)

>> OPTIONS <<
Routes 1(a) & 27 (a)

Mr Steele meets the "Ladies of Llangollen"

"A singular circumstance relates to the Character
of these two ladies: They swore eternal friendship
having experienced various misfortunes + troubles
in the World; they resolved never to disunite each
other, to live + die together; to sojourn in some
secluded spot remote from tumult, gaiety + bustle.
To accomplish this, their most desirable object,
they made a Tour through North + South Wales
purposely to explore and fix upon their future
abode where they might glean solace by an
alleviation of their troubles, where the pervading
cares that pester the mind may be exterminated +
subdued. By proper reflection we find solitude has
many charms. These ladies might with propriety
address Solitude with the following lines from
Shakespeare ......

"They at last fixed upon a Cottage in the Vale of
Llangothlin term'd Plas Nawydd [Plas Newydd] - a
Welsh signification for New Hall, which place
shall attempt a brief description.

"Plas Newydd is situated near the church. Upon our
approach to the Hall, the Ladies were in a most
affable and understanding manner, perfectly
according with their general demenour - desired
their Gardner to conduct us over their Grounds.
The Cottage itself is remarkably, nay singularly,
curious. The Portico, of which is all of carved
work, resembling Mahogany of great antiquity peaced
together. There are four Pillars, two on each side
the Doors. Formerly Bedposts, these pillars from
antiquity are a very great curiosity. The interior
of this cottage is a neatness itself.

" Lady Elenor + Miss Ponsonby are never seen either at home or abroad attired in any other habitments than Riding habit; their hair dressed and powdered, in every respect resembling the Man of fashion as far as respects Dress.

"There is a small lawn before the Cottage. After viewing and surveying minutely every particle of the exterior we walked over the Grounds, through which runs a Brook term'd Cuf-Lynmyn. In one part of these Gardens is a compact little Grotto in which is a small library of Books, the productions of the most renown'd Writers both Modern + Antient. Here these eccentric Ladies Resort to amuse their minds with the solace of reading. Near which stands another little Grotto in which observes an Hour Glass placed upon the centre of a Table, evidently serving as an Emblem of Time which never stops to suit the convenience of thought of Man. In this little retreat was a choice depository of Books likewise. Near which is a Well called Collan Well [after St Collen who founded Llangollen] the Water of which is produced from a Spring - in Welsh as term'd Catlyn.

"In another part of these Grounds is a beautiful Green house, the front of which consists of beautiful stained glass. Within are a great variety of the productions of nature. At the Extremity of these grounds, which are Romantic and Picturesque is a small Water Mill term'd Catlyn. These grounds, under the supervision of a Gardener are laid out in a very tastely manner abounding with the multifarious objects of Nature of various forms and hues, and interspersed in Regular order. Praise and credit upon the owners for their nice discrimination of taste."

3

Llangollen - Plas Newydd
.6 mile   1 km

Just a short link route to Plas Newydd so you can walk Routes 2, 4 & 6.

Plas Newydd to Llangollen

*

Llangollen to Plas Newydd

(1) Leaving Tourist Information Office, cross road & take street past front of Royal Hotel. Follow to A5 at Sun Inn.

(2) Cross & take Butler Hill up to entrance of

Plas Newydd
●
>> OPTIONS <<
Routes 2(a), 4(1) & 6(1)

(a) From Plas Newydd entrance go R down Butler Hill to A5.

ROUTE 5(2) RUNS R

(b) Take street opposite & follow to town centre.

Llangollen

>> OPTIONS <<
Routes 1(1), 5(1) 22(1), (B) & (C)

Mr Steele's dinner is unimproved by a Harper ....

" After descending this mountain we walk'd back to our Headquarters at Llangothlin where we found our Dinner prepared for us consisting of Stew'd Eels and Roast Ducks. We were favoured during dinner with the dubious sound of a Welsh Harp. The Harper performed several popular Welsh airs. Amongst his variety was pereformed the acknowleged favourite one "The Quarrel of Morgan and his wife". After Dinner and the enjoyment which Bacchus affords we walked about the Town and its environs. The principal Inns are the King's Head, Chirk Castle or Hand Inn close to which runs the River Dee. From here we walked into the churchyard - the River Dee beautifully winding on one side + mountains on all sides."

(22)

Plas Newydd

4

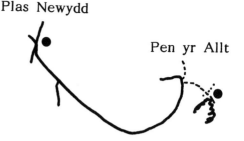

Pen yr Allt

Plas Newydd - Pen yr Allt
(Low Level Route)
1.8 miles 3 kms

This route follows a lane around the loop of Pengwern Vale. We include it to offer a low level alternative to the horrendously steep but much more interesting Route 6. You can wave to the more determined walkers taking it, who will be peering at you from the lower edge of the forest.

Look out for Pengwern Hall. An earlier building on the site is said to have been a Grange for Valle Crucis Abbey. The long driveway is private. Pengwern Vale (pen = head; gwern = marsh) was once a loop of the River Dee, carrying it south around Pen y Coed Hill.

Plas Newydd to Pen yr Allt
(Low Level)

(1) Put your back to Plas Newydd entrance & go L appx 2 mile (ignore lane & tracks off) to L bend & tracks R & ahead.

ROUTE 5(b) TAKES TRACK AHEAD

(2) Take track R, up via gate to power pole R.

Pen yr Allt
●
>> OPTIONS <<
Routes 5(a), 6(1), 7(1) & 14(a)

Pen yr Allt to Plas Newydd
(Low Level)

(a) From power pole by track, go DOWN to lane bend. Go L.

(b) Follow lane appx 2 miles

ROUTE 6(2) TAKES 1ST LANE L

to entrance of

Plas Newydd.
●
>> OPTIONS <<
Routes 2(a), 3(a) & 6(1)

5

Llangollen - Pen yr Allt
1.8 miles   3 kms

This route passes Ty'n Dwr YHA. Hostellers can join by walking 100 yds from hostel gates, then turning to paragraphs
(7) going to Pen yr Allt,
or (f) to Llangollen.

A charming route with a wood and a track on a brackeny hillside. Ty'n Dwr Youth Hostel is said to have had the oldest yew tree in Wales in its grounds in 1854. Is this the one still remaining?

Llangollen

Pen yr Allt

✱

Llangollen to Pen yr Allt

(1) Leaving Tourist Information Office, cross road & take street past front of Royal Hotel. Follow to A5 at Sun Inn.

(2) Go L to Star Inn & take Brook St opposite up to white railings L.

(3) Take path up to T junction, go L, pass cottage & take path R to stile (1).

(24)

(4) Go ahead, curve L past stile R, pass between walls, ignore L fork & take stile (2).

(5) Go ahead & take stile (3), ignore L fork & on to join wall R (ignore L fork) to take stile (4).

(6) Go ahead, pass 2 R forks, take stile (5) & on to lane.

Ty'n Dwr
(YHA gate 100yds R)

(7) Take stile opposite path & cross 2 fields via stile, to take stile.

(8) Go with hedge on your R & take gate to farm drive. Go R along barn wall & take middle white iron gate.

(9) Go ahead (via double gates if closed) to cross stream & take gate.

(10) Go ahead to end of wall R, then go R, paths becomes track, to lane corner with tracks.

ROUTE 4(b) TAKES LANE AHEAD

(11) Take track L, via gate, to power pole R.

Pen yr Allt
●
>> OPTIONS <<
Route 4(a), 6(a), 7(1) & 14(a)

Pen yr Allt to Llangollen

(a) From power pole by track go DOWN to lane bend.

(b) Take track R, stay by L fence to wall. Go L & take gate

(c) Cross stream & go ahead (via double gates if closed) & take white gate.

(d) Go ahead towards camp shop, at end of barn take gate L.

(e) Go ahead up field edge & take stile. Cross 2 fields via stile, to stile & lane.

Ty'n Dwr
(YHA gate 100yds L)

(f) Take path opposite stile & up to take stile (1). Keep to main path, pass path L & take stile (2).

(g) Ignore path L & R fork by wall, & on via stiles (3) & (4)

(h) Path goes between walls to grass. Go down with L hedge, pass stile L & curve R, then via stile (5) to path junction.

(i) Go L to junction & R to road. Go R to A5 & L to Sun Inn

ROUTE 3(2) GOES L UP
BUTLER HILL

Take street R to town centre.

Llangollen
●
>> OPTIONS <<
Routes 1(1), 3(1), 22(1),
(B) & (C)
(B) & (C)

Pen yr Allt

Plas Newydd

6

Plas Newydd - Pen yr Allt
(High Level)
2.7 mile   4.5 km

This exciting route jumps 900 feet up to 1150 feet
in about a mile. The climb is breathtaking but so
are the views.

Almost at your feet a lane curves along the bottom
of Pengwern Vale, which was once a loop of the
River Dee. This is Route 4 and you can shout
remarks at the low level walkers using it.

Due south you can see the limestone escarpment
wrapped around the base of Ruabon Mountain. The
nearest part is known as Trevor Rocks. The
steepling hill of Dinas Bran is a little to the
left; oddly, it can be difficult to see against the
mountain background. Further left are the sculpted
brown tops of Llantysilio and Maesyrchen Mountains,
the highest being Moel Gamelin at about 1800 feet.

Blue and hazy to the east, you may see the
Froncysyllte Aqueduct and the Cheshire Plain.

Plas Newydd to Pen yr Allt
(High Level)

(1) Leaving Plas Newydd, go L, cross bridge & take 2nd lane R.

(2) Climb appx .6 mile to enter wood & reach footpath sign R, opposite forest track L.

(3) Cross fence R by the FP sign, & go up with forest on your L to its end.

(4) Take BOTH gates & go with fence on your L. Nearing field corner, bear R & take stile to road.

(5) Go L, pass lane R & cross junction, then appx 100 yds to end of field L, & take gate L.

(6) Go with hedge on your R, becomes track, & down via gates appx .75 mile. Pass 2 tracks R to power pole L.

Pen yr Allt

●

>> OPTIONS <<
Routes 4(a) 5(a), 7(1) & 14(a)

Pen yr Allt to Plas Newydd
(High Level)

(a) From power pole go UP with wood on your R & follow track appx .75 mile to road.

(b) Go R appx .3 mile, thro cross roads & past lane L, to take stile R.

(c) Bear R to join fence to follow to field corner. Take BOTH gates.

(d) Go down with forest on your R, (crossing sheep fence via sort of stile) to bottom field corner. Cross fence R to lane.

(e) Go down L appx .6 mile to join lane from R

ROUTE 4(1) RUNS R

Go L. Cross stream & on to Plas Newydd entrance R.

Plas Newydd

>> OPTIONS <<
Routes 2(a) & 3(a)

Pen yr Allt

7

 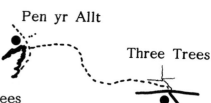

Three Trees

Pen yr Allt - Three Trees
1.35 miles   2 kms

The views from this grass track are sensational, gradually revealed if you are climbing, or changing perspective if coming down. The three trees have long since been replaced by three signposts.

To the northwest are the brown peaks of Llantysilio Mountain and across the Vale the squatting bulk of Ruabon Mountain, bandaged by that terrific limestone escarpment. Between them but closer, Dinas Bran towers over Llangollen town. To the east across the Cheshire Plain, you may see the spiney ridge of the Peckforton Hills, with Beeston Hill and its castle at the north end. And further north, on a clear day, you can make out the sandstone wedge of Helsby Hill on the River Mersey.

The track may have Roman origins, so if you glimpse a glint of metal and the red uniforms of the 20th Legion, or a team of mules burdened with mediaeval goods for English cities, do not worry. They are just the vibrations of former walkers.

Pen yr Allt to Three Trees

(1) From power pole go UP appx 150 yds & take L fork.

(2) Follow appx 1.25 miles to tarmac lane & three road signs.

●

Three Trees
>> OPTIONS <<
Routes 8(a) & 10(a)

Three Trees to Pen yr Allt

(a) From T junction of lanes & 3 signs, take gate & follow grass track appx 1.25 mile to track junction at wood edge.

(b) Go R 150 yds to power pole.

●

Pen yr Allt
>> OPTIONS <<
Routes 4(a), 5(a), 6(a) & 14(a)

8

Ty'n y Groes - Three Trees
1.3 miles   2 kms

A walk along a quiet lane. At about 1200 feet, Three Trees is the second highest point in this network of walks. In winter, when the rest of the Vale is seeing the end of snow and ice, these roads are still frozen, with cold drifting mists. One can hardly believe civilization is only a mile away.

Three Trees

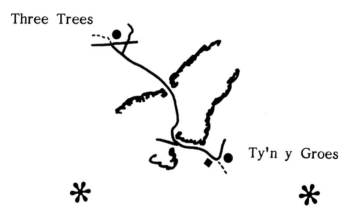

Ty'n y Groes

*

Ty'n y Groes to Three Trees

(1) At cottages & gate on lane bend, put your back to gate, then go L & take 1st lane R.

(2) Follow appx 1 mile, cross junction of track & lane, to T junction with gate & 3 road signs.

Three Trees
●
>> OPTIONS <<
Routes 7(a) & 10(a)

*

Three Trees to Ty'n y Groes

(a) At T junction of lanes & 3 road signs, take lane opposite gate.

(b) Follow appx 1 mile to fork & go L to cottages on lane bend.

Ty'n y Groes
●
>> OPTIONS <<
Routes 9(a) & 11(1)

A delightful walk through sheep cropped parkland, with fine beech trees, oaks, ash and chestnuts. The ground rises towards the castle, which is strangely squat from this low angle view.

9

Chirk - Ty'n y Groes
2.3 miles 3.7 kms

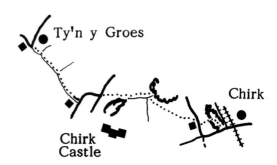

Ty'n y Groes

Chirk

Chirk
Castle

Chirk to Ty'n y Groes

(1) From station car park, go R over railway & canal & take stile R.

(2) Take path thro wood (either fork), & exit via stile. Go up midfield to stile & lane.

[To see castle gates
go 200 yds L]

(2) Go R a few paces & take track by timber framed cottage. Take gate & follow white topped posts to join castle drive, & on to junction by farm.

[Go L to visit castle.]

(3) Go R, take stile on R of farm & follow white topped posts to lane by cottages.

●

Ty'n y Groes
>> OPTIONS <<
Routes 8(1) & 11(1)

Ty'n y Groes to Chirk

(a) From cottages on bend of lane, take stile & follow white topped posts past farm to castle drive.

[Go R to visit castle.]

(b) Go L to drive junction, take stile & carry on with white topped posts to lane.

[To see castle gates
go 200 yds R]

(c) Go R a few paces & take stile L. Go down midfield & take stile into wood.

(d) Take either fork & follow path to lane. Go L to station.

●

Chirk.
>> OPTION <<
Route (H)

(30)

Chirk Castle has been continuously inhabited since it was built for Sir Roger Mortimer, one of Edward I's commanders, who was given the newly created lordship of Chirkland to protect the border against future rebellions. Sir Roger soon became Justiciar of all Wales but his ambitions finally landed him in the Tower of London, where he ended his days.

The castle treasures include gifts of furniture from Sir Francis Drake to the Myddleton family, whose descendants still live here. Guide books for the castle and gardens are available at the entrance.

The magnificent wrought iron gates are the work of two brothers who lived on the castle estate at Croesfoel near Wrexham during the 18th century.

10

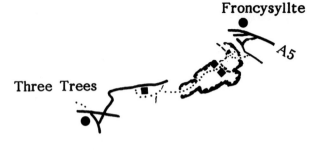

Three Trees

Froncysyllte

A5

Froncysyllte - Three Trees
1.8 miles 3 kms

A truly splendid walk rising nearly 500 feet from
the Vale to the tops. From Three Trees you have a
huge panorama from the Cheshire Plain in the east
to Llangollen and Llantysilio Mountain in the west.
There is a precipice path above a limestone quarry,
through pink flowering dog roses with wild flowers
underfoot. In June, the quarry walls are crimson
with valerian; as I walked down a buzzard
soared out over the abyss.

✱

Froncysllte to Three Trees

(1) Put your back to Aqueduct
Inn & go L. Cross A5 & take
Methodist's Hill R.

(2) Ignore 1st lane R & climb
to pass 2nd R by phone box. Go
on appx 100yds & take path R.

(3) Follow wood path, ignore 2
paths R, to T junction at wire
fence.

(4) Go L to track, go L & round
R bend to junction.

(5) Cross track & take track
ahead   between   houses   to
mysterious squat brick thing.

(6) Go R to pass it & follow
rising path past precipice L,
then on R. At limestone pits,
pass them on your R.

(7) Continue on main path via
stile (becomes green lane, &
small gate, to exit past house
R to lane.

(8) Go up L to junction, then R
to next junction by 3 signs.

Three Trees
●

>> OPTIONS <<
Routes 7(a) & 8(a)

(32)

✱ Three Trees to Froncysllte

(a) At T junction of lanes by 3 signs, put your back to gate & go L to junction.

(b) Go L to 1st house R. Take path past R of house (ignore small path R to shed) & along house wall. (Nettles soon go.)

(c) Follow green lane via small gate to take stile.

(d) Ignore wood edge path L & go on to open area with limestone pits L. ◥

(e) Curve R past pits, follow precipice path & pass house L to track.

(f) Cross, take track opposite & twist L & down a few paces, to take path R by TV gizmo.

(g) Go along wire fence appx 20 yds, then R on woodland path. Pass 2 paths L, to lane.

(h) Go L to phone box, fork R & down to A5 & Aqueduct Inn.

●
Froncysyllte
>> OPTIONS <<
Routes 14(1), (F) or (G)

Mr Steele describes the Aqueduct;

" ..... a road which brought us to the aqueduct. We put up our chaise at a small public house called the Travers Arms where you have an excellent view of the Aqueduct, one of the greatest specimens of the works of Man and Art I ever beheld. It's built over the River Dee; upon the top of which runs a Canal navigable for coal Barges. It consists of 20 arches - each Column, 18 in number, support the Bridge, which are of Cast Iron, every column being built with Stone, 4 of which are 44 yards in height. These 4 have their foundations in the breadth of the River. The basement of each Column is square.

From a stone which I sat on close beside the River to view the height of the Aqueduct; turn my eyes which way, I would observe nothing but an obscure and almost unfrequented Vale - our only companions an immense number of Trees of various heights and dimensions, which have stood the blasts of ages."

(33)

11 Ty'n y Groes - Irish Bridge
2.2 miles   3.5 kms

This route follows the Offa's Dyke Path along
narrow crooked lanes. From the higher section near
Ty'n y Groes, there are some views of the Cheshire
Plain to the east. Near Irish Bridge it follows
the line of the Dyke for a spell, a long bank
topped with a gappy hedge.

Ty'n y Groes   A5   Irish Bridge

Irish Bridge was named after the Irish navvies who
laboured and toiled, away from their native land
and without JCB's or Guinness, to cut this long
narrow ditch. They finished in 1805.

In many places railways started to eclipse canals
within 35 years, but special factors applied to
this cut. Slow development of railways in Wales
allowed the Shropshire Union Canal system as a
whole, including the Welsh bits, to prosper right
up to 1914. A key factor was the major share
-holding of the London & North Western Railway,
which was happy to let the canal company flourish,
since it gave them a long arm into Great Western
territory.

Nearby is what must be the forerunner to the
motorway, Telford's London - Hollyhead road, the
A5, which never exceeds his specified maximum
gradient of 1 in 22.

T'n y Groes to Irish Bridge

(1) At lane bend by cottages, put your back to gate/stile & go R.

(2) Follow lane appx .3 mile, past belt of trees, to next R corner. Take stile under oak L

(3) Cross to L of hawthorn & take 2 stiles. Sight conifers ahead L of farm, make for their L end & take stile to track.

(4) Go R to lane, then L. At fork go R, go over crossroads to next R bend & junction L.

(5) Take stile R, bear R across field corner & via gap to next field. Go down diagonally, & via stile & field edge to A5.

(5) Go R a few paces & take track L to field. Follow bank on R. As field starts to fall, go R thro hedge gap & down 2 narrow fields to stile, A483 & canal bridge.

Irish Bridge
●
>> OPTIONS <<
Routes 12(1), (G) & (H)

Irish Bridge to Ty'n y Groes

(a) From canal bridge on A483, take stile on non towpath side. Go length of 2 fields, take stile & hedge gap.

(b) Go L & join track to A5. Go R a few paces, cross & take stile.

(c) Follow field edge & take stile, then up diagonally, appx 5 yds L of power pole, to field corner. Take hedge gap & bear L across field corner to stile to lane.

(d) Go L, over cross roads & past lane R, to farm L.

(e) Take track opposite farm, cross stile L. Go ahead, slowly drawing closer to L hedge to take corner stiles.

(f) Make for biggest oak & take stile to lane. Go R to lane bend by cottages & track.

Ty'n y Groes
●
>> OPTIONS <<
Routes 8(1) & 9(a)

There is a fair stretch of road in this route but we thought you would put up with it for the rather nice Country Park. This is our only Deeside walk, with a viaduct at one end and the Pontcysyllte aqueduct at the other. There are interesting views from the road.

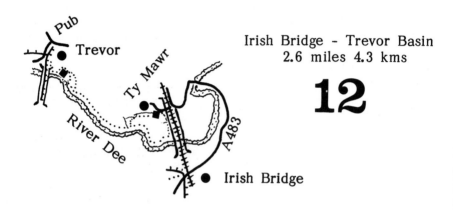

Irish Bridge - Trevor Basin
2.6 miles 4.3 kms

12

Ty Mawr Country Park was developed by Wrexham Maelor Borough Council on the steep grassy south bank of the Dee. The gigantic Newbridge Viaduct strides across one side and the Pontcysyllte Aqueduct is in sight to the west. In spite of its height, the lines of Telford's aqueduct are softened by trees and the black cast iron trough looks friendly. It does not mind the people in shorts and the boats, strolling and bumbling. By contrast, the viaduct has an almost inhuman perfection. Look up from near the river at those precision masonry arches chomping across the sky.

The park is ideal for children. It has Jacob's sheep, ducks, geese, hens, goats, ponies and donkies. However there is also space to sit and contemplate on wooden seats by the river. For details of events contact the park rangers on 0978 822780.

(36)

*

Irish Bridge to Trevor Basin

(1) From canal bridge on A483, cross railway & follow road 1.3 miles & cross Dee to junction.

(2) Go L under railway & on to Country Park entrance L.

Ty Mawr

(3) From buildings, take stile in R corner of car park. Follow stone path, curves down to river & FP sign by stile R.

(4) Take stile & path to fork, go either way to stone track.

(5) Go L over bridge, pass R of building to aqueduct & take steps up to canal basin.

Trevor Basin
●
>> OPTIONS <<
Routes 13(1), 15(1), (E) & (F)

*

Trevor Basin to Irish Bridge

(a) In canal basin get on non shop side & head for aqueduct. Just before it take path L & follow steps to river.

(b) Go downstream past building & on stone track to bridge.

(c) Cross & go R on either field path, follow along & on take stile.

(d) Follow river path to viaduct, then L beside it & exit via stile to track, & up to Country Park entrance.

Ty Mawr

(e) At park entrance go R, pass under railway.

(f) Go R appx 1.3 miles across Dee, then railway, to canal bridge.

Irish Bridge
●
>> OPTIONS <<
Routes 11(a), (G) & (H)

Newbridge Viaduct

From this pretty lane you have a river level view of the mellow stone Cysylltau Bridge, built in the light grained local Cefn y Fedw Sandstone. And you can see two interesting properties which are both private houses. One is Trevor Old Mill which has been restored by the owner and has the largest overshot water wheel in Wales. The other is Plas yn Pentre, which has a priest hole hidden in the wall and another in the roof.

Trevor Basin - Bryn Howel
1.7 miles   2.8 kms

13

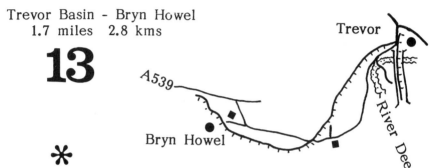

*

Trevor Basin to Bryn Howel

(1) In canal basin get on non shop side & head for aqueduct, but take path R before it down to stone wall R.

(2) Go R, under aqueduct, to lane & down L to river bridge. DON'T CROSS.

(3) Follow lane appx 1.5 miles; crossing canal at half way, & appx .5 mile on, take track L to canal bridge. (Bryn Howel Hotel is to R.)

Bryn Howel
●
>> OPTIONS <<
Routes (D) & (E)

*

Bryn Howel to Trevor Basin

(a) From towpath cross bridge & follow track R to lane.

(b) Go R appx 1.5 miles, via canal bridge, to lane junction & stone river bridge.

(c) DON'T CROSS, go up L & take path R under aqueduct, then up L to canal basin.

Trevor Basin
●
>> OPTIONS <<
Routes 12(a), 15(1), (F) & (E)

(39)

Lift Bridge at Froncysyllte

14 Froncysyllte - Pen yr Allt
2.5 miles   4 kms

This route climbs gently from canal level up the southern side of the Vale. At Froncysyllte a series of lanes and village footpaths leads past gardens and chapels and a nature reserve. The rest is a long track through the forest. Froncysyllte means brow of Cysyllte. There is no easy translation but the name suggests the place where two rock landforms meet in a valley.

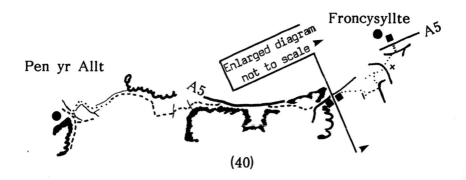

Froncysyllte to Pen yr Allt

(1) From bus shelter by Aqueduct Inn, cross A5 to iron railings & take steps.

(2) At top go R & take rising paved path with rubber grips. Go on past seat R to lane bend.

(3) Go L a few paces & take track R, becomes path, to path junction.

(4) Go L to lane bend, go R & take 1st track R to nature reserve gate.

(5) Take path R to lane. Go L, pass 4 houses L, & on appx 200 yds to gap in railings R. Take track R down to A5.

(6) Go L appx 300 yds & take forest track L (becomes path) appx 1 mile.

(7) Track passes thro steel gate & a few yards on to field corner. Go R to ruin L.

(8) Go L thro ruin. Take gate--way thro wall to grass track.

(9) Go L & fork R down to track junction, with power pole R.

Pen yr Allt
●
>> OPTIONS <<
Routes 4(a), 5(a), 6(a) & 7(1)

Pen yr Allt to Froncysyllte

(a) From power pole by track, go UP a few paces & at wood corner R, take grass track L.

(b) Curve up L to trees & wall & take gateway R.

(c) Go thro ruin to corner of wall L with hawthorns, & take path R along field edge.

(d) Round field corner & take gate. Go with fence on your L & follow track appx 1 mile to A5.

(e) Go R, pass track L & on appx 150 yds, to corner of wood R. Take path R to lane.

(f) Go L, pass 3 houses R & after of garden of 4th, take path R to nature reserve gate. Go L to lane.

(h) Go L to R bend, take path L to path junction. Go R to lane opposite chapel.

(i) Cross lane to L & pass seat L. Join path L with rubber grips down to lane.

(j) Go on a few paces & take steps L to A5 & Aqueduct Inn.

Froncysyllte
●
>> OPTIONS <<
Routes 10(1), (F) & (G)

15

Trevor Basin - Monument
1.8 miles 3 kms

This route follows the Offa's Dyke Path, rising from 60 feet at river level to about 1100 feet in just under two miles. A walk through the black bowels of a conifer wood separates the green valley scenery from the limestone tops, where you have views of the whole Vale of Llangollen.

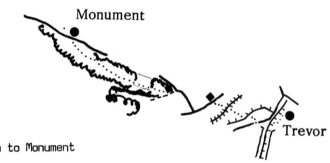

Monument

Trevor

*

Trevor Basin to Monument

(1) In canal basin get on non shop side & head for aqueduct, but take path R before it down to stone wall. Go R   under aqueduct to lane.

(2) Go down L to postbox R & take path by it up to canal. Cross & follow field path to old railway.

(3) Go L & under, then R & round L bend to A539.

(3) Go L & take 1st lane R. Round L bend to R bend by house.

(4) Take track ahead appx 100 yds to stile R. Cross or pass it (!) to follow path thro wood, up field edge & thro forest to stile & lane.

(Monument is opposite appx 200 yds up on L.)

Monument
●
>> OPTIONS <<
Routes 17(1) & 18(a)

(42)

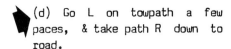

(a) From road take stile & follow path thro forest, down field edge & thro wood to stone track.

(b) Go L, join lane & follow to A 539.

(c) Go L to 1st house L & take path opposite. Pass under old railway & follow field path to cross canal.

(d) Go L on towpath a few paces, & take path R down to road.

Go up L & take path R under viaduct, then up L to canal basin.

Trevor Basin
●
>> OPTIONS <<
Routes 12(a), 13(1) (E) & (F)

16

Nyth y Dryw - Sun Trevor
.6 mile 1 km

Just a short and simple link route using a road or the canal, and a track so hidden it might almost be a secret.

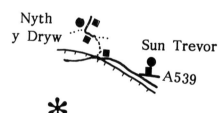

Nyth y Dryw

Sun Trevor

A539

Nyth y Dryw to Sun Trevor

(1) From bend of lane by gate go DOWN lane to A539.

(2) Go L on road or canal towpath to Inn

Sun Trevor
●
>> OPTIONS <<
Routes (D) & (C)

Sun Trevor to Nyth y Dryw

(a) From Sun Inn, cross A539 to canal & go L on towpath to bridge.

(b) Get onto road & go R a few paces, then cross & take grass track L of garage.

(c) Pass house R to next sharp R bend with gate.

Nyth y Dryw
●
>> OPTIONS <<
Routes 17(a), 19(a) 20(a)

(43)

Central Group of Routes
17, 18, 19

You can see from the map that these three share the same lanes, but the diagram shows quite clearly which is which. Just use the one you want and forget about the others.

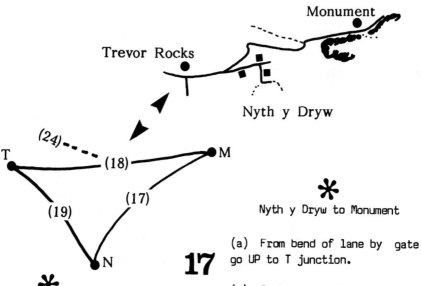

Monument

Trevor Rocks

Nyth y Dryw

*
Nyth y Dryw to Monument

(a) From bend of lane by gate go UP to T junction.

(b) Go L to junction, then R appx 1 mile.

AT 2ND SHARP BEND OPPOSITE SEAT R, ROUTE 24(Mb) RUNS L UP GRASS TRACK

(c) When woods start on R go on to stile R.

(Monument is L & behind you appx 200 yds up hill.)

Monument
●
>> OPTIONS <<
Route 15(a) & 24(Ma)

*
Monument to Nyth y Dryw

(1) Face stile on wood edge. Go R on road appx 1 mile, to junction.

(2) Go sharp L & down past house R to house L.

(3) Take track R past house L to sharp L bend with gate R.

Nyth y Dryw
●
>> OPTIONS <<
Routes 16(1) & 20(a)

17

* Trevor Rocks to Monument

18   *****

(1) From cattle grid where lane meets road, face road & go R appx 1.5 miles (go L at fork).

Monument to Trevor Rocks

AT 2ND SHARP BEND OPPOSITE SEAT R, ROUTE 24(Mb) RUNS L UP GRASS TRACK.

(a) At stile onto road, face stile & go R appx 1.5 miles, past 1st junction L to 2nd with cattle grid.

(2) Pass where woods start on R & go on to stile R.

Trevor Rocks
●

Monument

>> OPTIONS <<
Routes 21(a) & 24(Ta)

>> OPTIONS <<
Route 15(a) & 24(Ma)

The Sun Trevor (formerly Sun Inn) is a coaching inn dating from the time when visitors to the Vale arrived by horse and chaise - like Mr Steele. Be sure to catch the view of Dinas Bran from east of the canal bridge. Trevor Rocks is part of the Eglwyseg Escarpment, so called because the quarrymen were from Trevor.

* **19**

Trevor Rocks to Nyth y Dryw

*

Nyth y Dryw to Trevor Rocks

(1) From cattle grid where lane meets road, face road & go R to fork.

(a) From bend of lane by gate go UP to T junction.

(2) Go R & pass house R to house L. Take track R, pass house L to next L bend with gate R.

(b) Go L to junction, then ahead to next junction with cattle grid L.

Trevor Rocks
●

Nyth y Dryw
●

>> OPTIONS <<
Routes 21(a) & 24(Ta)

>> OPTIONS <<
Routes 16(1) & 20(a)

(45)

Offa's Dyke Path in the Limestone

The lane between the Monument and Trevor Rocks is
known as the Panorama Walk and follows the Offa's
Dyke Path. You will also meet the ODP on its way
through the Vale of Llangollen on Routes 24, 15,
G, 12 and 11.

The Offa's Dyke Path runs 173 miles between
Chepstow on the Bristol Channel and Prestatyn on
the North Wales coast. More or less, it follows the
line of the great earthwork ordered by the Saxon
King Offa of Mercia (757 - 796), for the purpose of
keeping the Welsh where he thought they belonged.

The Path was one of the early Long Distance
Footpaths. Starting as an idea by a group of
enthusiasts, it was taken up by the Countryside
Commission in 1955 and officially opened in 1971.
It is an epic walk through a rolling green
landscape, treading the Clywydian Hills, the Severn
Valley, the Clun and Radnor Forests, the Black
Mountains, and the Wye Valley.

(46)

Llangollen was originally a settlement of St Collen (llan = church or church land, gollen = Collen). The town is now a popular country resort for visitors with many different pursuits in mind. In winter the town is flooded with white water canoeists. In spring daytrippers from Merseyside are in abundance. Summer brings the holiday traffic, often on its way to Snowdonia or Ireland. For walkers the favourite season is the autumn when the Vale is lit by the golden hues of birch on the hillside. Eating places in the town include vegetarian, Indian, Chinese and pizza with a variety of coffee and afternoon tea shops.

The town is best known for its annual International Eisteddfod. For one week in every July since 1947, singers, dancers and musicians from all over the world have come to compete and give concerts. There are competitions for choirs of children and adults, soloists and quartets, including "Choir of the Year, "Soloist of the Year" and "Choir of the World". Celebrity artists have joined in, such as Yehudi Menhuin, Joan Sutherland and Placido Domingo. The motto of the Eisteddfod is "Byd gwyn fydd byd a gano, gwariadd fydd ei gerddi fo." (Blessed is a world that sings, gentle are its songs.)

It is no coincidence that the town also supports ECTARC - European for Centre for Traditional and Regional Cultures, which was established in 1983. At its converted chapel in Castle Street, ECTARC has a conference hall and both permanent and temporary exhibitions, all aimed at raising awareness of the variety of cultures within Europe. The centre has the largest Arthurian library in the world. Entrance is free.

20

Four Ways - Nyth y Dryw
1.3 miles   2 kms

A very pleasant walk with a path on the edge of a
wood, two farms and a fine midfield group of oak
and ash trees. There is a steep little valley
making a very pretty setting for one of the farms.
You could meet an apparently insane but harmless
ram that runs madly about in all directions.

Four Ways   Nyth y Dryw

*   Four Ways to Nyth y Dryw

(1) From junction of three
tracks & lane, take track
opposite lane.

(2) Pass houses R, enter fields
& follow upper edges to lane.

(3) Cross & take stile L of
gate. Go with hedge on your R &
take gate.

(4) Go half L over field & take
stile. Go L & take stile by
small gate.

(5) Go down with hedge on your
R to corner, then R & take
stile to paddock.

(6) Cross midfield & take
stile, then stile L & up yard
to exit via gate. Follow track
appx 150 yds & take stile R.

(7) Make for R side of midfield
oaks & follow path thro line of
trees. Keep same level & curve
L to take stile.

(6) Go up rough track to gate &
bend of lane.

Nyth y Dryw
●
>> OPTIONS <<
Routes 16(1), 17(a) & 19(a)

(48)

Nyth y Dryw to Four Ways

(a) From bend of lane, take gate. Ignore gate/gap R & follow rough track down to take stile.

(b) Bear L into trees & follow them, curving R on same level, then head for farm & take stile to track.

(c) Go L, thro yard & take stile. Cross drive R & take stile to paddock.

(d) Cross & take corner stile. Follow grass track to fence corner, then up L & take stile.

(e) Go half R & take gate, then with hedge on your R to stile & lane.

(f) Cross, take small gate opposite & follow upper field edges to join track. Follow to junction of 3 tracks & lane.

Four Ways

●

>> OPTIONS <<

Routes 21(1), 22(a) & 23(1)

Quarry at Trevor Rocks and Dinas Bran

(49)

21 Four Ways - Trevor Rocks
.9 mile   1.5 km

Castell Dinas Bran was built on the site of an Iron Age Hill fort; the embankments can still be seen. The stone castle may have been built in the mid 13th century by the Prince of Powys. See what Mr Steele has to say about it.

At the north end of this route is the escarpment known as Trevor Rocks. There are no definitive paths onto it, although many walkers find access points along the road.

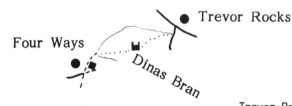

Trevor Rocks

Four Ways

Trevor Rocks to Four Ways

* Four Ways to Trevor Rocks

(1) From junction of 3 tracks & lane, take track so as to pass corner house on your R & take kissing gate.

(2) Turn half R & make for summit & Castell Dinas Bran.

(3) Face the escarpment, then go down half R & take stile to lane. Go up L to cattle grid.

Trevor Rocks
●

>> OPTIONS <<
Routes 18(1), 19(1) & 24(Ta)

(a) At junction of lane & road, cross cattle grid & go DOWN lane to take stile R.

(b) Make for summit & Castell Dinas Bran.

(c) Face town & go half right down zig zag path, near bottom ignore stile L & cross hump to corner gates.

(d) Take kissing gate & go to junction of 3 tracks & lane.

Four Ways

>> OPTIONS <<
Routes 20(1), 22(a) & 23(1)

Mr Steele ascends Castell Dinas Bran ...

"From here we ascended a Mountain term'd Croak
Castle - otherwise Castle Dinas Bran near which
are the Elusig Rocks [Eglwyseg Escarpment and
Trevor Rocks]: remarkably curious, almost
resembling Mountains cover'd with Snow. At the
bottom of this mountain is the Seat of McCunliffe
who married the daughter of Lord Crag. Castle Dinas
Bran is the highest mountain about this part of
Wales [of course it isn't, both Ruabon Mountain
north of the Escarpment and the Berwyn to the
south are higher].

I ascended the top with considerable difficulty being
unaccustomed to climb Mountains I did not ascend with
the agility of a Monkey. Having reached its summit I
felt disposed to rest + refresh myself by reclining
upon a Mossy Couch. After the abatement of fatigue I
indulged myself by viewing and contemplating the
surrounding and almost unparalled prospect of a
magnificent amphitheatre of Mountains, some as remote
as Derbyshire. The grandeur of the scene most amply
repaid me for the fatigue + toil I experienced in
accomplishing my purpose and desire. The village of
Llangothlin [his earlier spelling is correct but
Steele seems to have been trying to anglicise the
Welsh he had heard since his arrival] from this great
eminence resembles a Town almost covered in Snow from
the houses being plastered over [and limewashed no
doubt].

At the top of this Mountain are the remains of an
immense Castle, which Castle originally was
inhabited by some Welsh Chieftains [the princes of
Powys] and their army stationed there for the purpose
of checking the designs or preventing an approach of
an Enemy out of England onto their own Territory,
being a considerable fortification commanding an
excellent view from Wales into England."

(51)

22

Llangollen - Four Ways
.4 mile .7 km

A short link route between Llangollen and Dinas Bran which is steeper than it seems, climbing 200 feet in no time.

*

Llangollen to Four Ways

(1) From Tourist Information Office, cross river & go R to end of hotel, then up L to cross canal.

(2) Take path opposite, cross lane & follow field edge up to track. Go on to junction of 3 tracks & lane.

Four Ways
●
>> OPTIONS <<
Routes 20(1), 21(1) & 23(1)

*

Four Ways to Llangollen

(a) From junction of 3 tracks & lane, take TRACK (not lane) DOWN & take gate R to field.

(b) Go down field edge, cross lane & take gate. Follow path to cross canal bridge & enter town.

Llangollen
●
>> OPTIONS <<
Routes (B), (C), 1(1), 3(1) & 5(1)

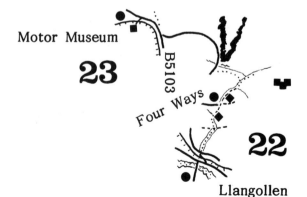

Motor Museum

23

B5103

Four Ways

22

Llangollen

A short route linking the foot of Dinas Bran to the Llangollen Canal. Quiet, mainly lane.

The Motor Museum holds a collection of British cars of the 1930's, 40's and 50's, all roadworthy and in regular summer use. Restoration work goes on around the visitor, in an old fashioned garage atmosphere. And the staff are keen to help customers keep their old cars going. If you need a widget for your Singer, Jowett or Sunbeam, try the spares section; they have 350 different kinds of sparking plug. The Museum is open almost all year.

Four Ways - Motor Museum
.9 mile   1.5 kms

23

Four Ways to Motor Museum

(1) From junction of 3 tracks & lane, go UP track to pass corner house on your R, & take gate.

(2) Go with fence on your L appx 350 yds to take stile L.

(3) Go down field edge & take stile to lane, then R appx .5 mile to B5103.

(4) Go R & cross canal bridge L to

Motor Museum
●
>> OPTIONS <<
Routes 25(1) (A) & (B)

Motor Museum to Four Ways

(a) From museum cross canal bridge to B5103. Go R past wood L & take lane L.

(b) Follow appx .5 mile, past lane L, then wood. Pass 1st stile & footpath sign. Go on to stream & take 2nd stile L to field.

(c) Go up field edge & take corner stile. Go R along fence & take gate.

ROUTE 21(2) RUNS TO SUMMIT

(d) Follow track to junction of 3 tracks & lane.

Four Ways
●
>> OPTIONS <<
Routes 20(1), 21(1) & 22(a)

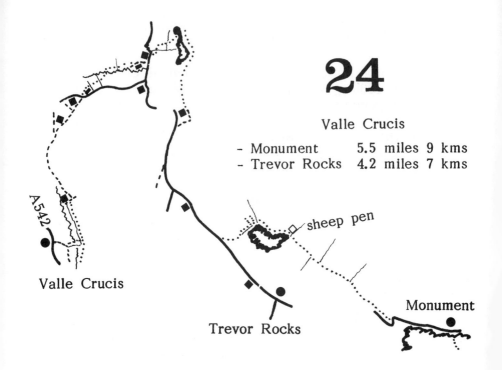

24

Valle Crucis

- Monument   5.5 miles 9 kms
- Trevor Rocks   4.2 miles 7 kms

Valle Crucis

sheep pen

Trevor Rocks

Monument

From Valle Crucis the way seems level, but it climbs slowly towards the head of the peaceful Eglwyseg Valley. Only at the end of the woodland do you see the terrific slope on the west side. There are some herb rich meadows full of wild flowers, very unusual in these days of reseeding and herbicides. Turning south, you join the the Offa's Dyke Path, grand and scenic through the limestone.

The northern leg of the route to the Monument involves a steep scramble on a limestone staircase, and from the crest at about 1300 feet are the grandest views of all. Here you are above Dinas Bran and the next highest point in the network, Three Trees at about 1150 feet. To the south west are the brown Berwyns and in the east the Cheshire Plain. On a clear day you may be able to see the Wrekin.

This is our longest and most varied route with alternative start or finishing points at one end. We are grateful to Mr Wynn Roberts for permission to cross his field near the sheep pen.

People who feel nervous about a rock scramble (quite small), are wearing high heels, are tired, have toothache etc, are advised to take to sweatless route to Trevor Rocks. You could then follow Route 18 to the Monument.

✱ Valle Crucis to Monument OR Trevor Rocks

(1) From A452, approach Abbey. At ticket office take gate L to caravan site.

(2) Go R on track, round L bend, then R over grass to cross bridge.

(3) Take path ahead to top of bank. Go L along field edges to track by cottage.

(4) Go R & thro gate. Go L on track appx .75 mile (fork R at Hendre) to lane.

(5) Go L, pass house R & take 1st gate R.

(6) Go ahead bearing a little L & take hedge gap to next field. Keep same line with bank on your R, bearing a little L to take gateway.

(7) Bear a bit L to point where fence meets stream. Cross via sort of stepping stones. ◣

(8) Go R along stream & cross fence nearest to it. Go half L a few paces to path.

(9) Go R, pass house R, via stile to track. Follow to lane.

(10) Go L to L bend & take stile R. Follow field path round L & take gate.

(11) Go up half R to hit hedge appx 100 yds from its R end, & take gap by waymark post.

(12) Keep appx same line bearing more L, to wood edge & find next waymark post.

(13) Take path into wood appx 32 paces, then go L & take stile. Go R with fence & round L bend up to join path.

(14) Go R following waymarks appx .7 mile, past farm R, to track, gate & lane.

(15) Go L appx .5 mile (pass lane R) to cattle grid & farm R ◣

Choose Monument or Trevor Rocks. Paragraphs to Monument now have M prefix, and to Trevor Rocks, T.)

✳ To Trevor Rocks

(T16) Follow lane appx 1 more mile to lane R with cattle grid.

Trevor Rocks
●
>> OPTIONS <<
Routes 18(1), 19(1) & 21(a)

✳ To Monument

(M16) Follow lane appx .3 mile counting (sorry about this) 11 telegraph poles. (If sums not up to this without calculator, look for 1st gate R - recessed in wall.)

(M17) A few paces after pole & opposite gate, take grass path diagonally R up hillside.

(M18) Stays clear into gorse, watch for fork & go up L under hawthorn to cleft & stream.

(M19) Go up with stream on your R, then old wall/fence to meet cross path.

(M20) Go R a few paces & resume line up. Cross path & on to take stile.

(M21) Go R with fence to its end. Keep same line (via stile by sheep pen) down green track appx 1.3 miles to lane.

(M22) Go L, pass end of wood R, to stile R.

Monument
●
>> OPTIONS <<
Routes 15(a), 17(1) & 18(a)

✳ Monument OR Trevor Rocks to Valle Crucis

(Paragraphs from Monument lettered as normal with M prefix, and that from Trevor Rocks with T.)

✳
(Ma) At MONUMENT, face stile by road & go R. Pass end of wood L to start of sharp L bend.

(Mb) Take grass track up ahead appx 1 mile & via stile by sheep pen to fenced plantation.

(Mc) Go with fence on your L to plantation end & take stile L.

(Md) Go down with fence on your L, cross 1st path to 2nd. Go R a few paces & resume line down.

(Me) Keep stream on your L down to cleft at bottom of rock staircase.

(56)

(Mf) Look R, note near hawthorn on same level & pass ABOVE it. Follow path down diagonally to lane.

(Mg) Go R appx .3 mile to cattle grid. (Next para (h).

****
*
(Ta) At TREVOR ROCKS face cattle grid & lane, then go R appx 1 mile to next cattle grid. (Next Para - (h).

****

(h) Follow lane appx .6 mile to gate & track R with Offa's Dyke sign.

(i) Follow track, round L bend, past house & across hillside to wood.

(j) Follow wood edge to cross stream. GREAT CARE. Wood falls away L, go appx 100 yds till it comes back & look down half L to see stile.

(k) Cross stile, go five paces then L to join clear path. Go R to wood edge.

(l) Sight far bottom field corner & make for hedge gap appx 100 yds up from it.

(m) Keep same line to take bottom field corner gate. Follow field track round R to stile & lane.

(n) Go L & take 1st gated track R. Follow til it bends L to house. Take path ahead & pass house on your L to take stile.

(o) Go appx 150 yds to 5 yds from fence corner. Take path L to stream & cross fence nearest to it.

(p) Count 170 paces along stream to where fences meet stream by 3 trunked sycamore.

(q) Cross via sort of stepping stones & go up half R to take gate.

(r) Cross midfield with bank on your L & take hedge gap to next field. Bear a little L & take corner gate on R of house, to lane.

(s) Go L between houses & take track R. Follow appx .75 mile to end.

(t) Take gate R & on to take gate L of cottage. Go with hedge on your R to its end. Go down R to cross bridge.

(u) Go ahead to join track & follow to Abbey entrance, then R to A452.

Valle Crucis
●
>> OPTIONS <<
Route 25(a) & 26(a)

(57)

25

Motor Museum - Valle Crucis
.6 mile 1 km

Valle Crucis Abbey ruin is open most of the year. It was built by the Cistercian (white) monks in the 13th century. At least two princes of Powys are buried here.

Valle Crucis

Motor Museum to Valle Crucis

Motor Museum

(1) From Museum cross canal bridge to B5103. Go R a few yards & cross to take 1st gate/stile L.

Valle Crucis to Motor Museum

(2) Follow field path to 2nd gate, then ahead to footpath sign.

ROUTE 24(3) RUNS R ON TOP OF BANK.

(3) Bear L along river & take footbridge.

(4) Go ahead to site road, then L to gate. Go R to A542.

(a) From A452 go to Abbey entrance & L into caravan site. Go R on site road, round L bend, then R to river & cross bridge.

(b) Go R along river & up bank to footpath sign. Cross field to take gate.

(c) Follow field path to A580. Go R & cross canal bridge to

Valle Crucis
●
>> OPTIONS <<
Routes 24(1) & 26(a)

Motor Museum
●
>> OPTIONS <<
Routes 23(a), (A) & (B)

Mr Steele inspects the Abby

"We walked to see the curious ruins of the Abby
Valle Cruces [Valle Crucis Abbey], distant 1 Mile +
half from Llangothlin, near the borders of
Mereonethshire. For some considerable distance we
passed between the River Dee and Canal - the Dee
on our left - + surrounded by Mountains. We cross a
bridge over the Canal which leaves them both upon
the left. We then come to Pentrovilla Bridge,
leaving on the left a mill call'd Pentrovilla Mill
[Pentrefelin]. We then come to the antiquated
remains of the Abby, formerly a monastry destroyed
by Henry 8th, if we may judge by the ruins it must
have been a very portly and spacious edifice.
There is a farmhouse attached to it, near which are
situated the Mountains Coad Hurdin [Coed Hyrddyn]
+ the Vromer. In one part of the Cloisters of this
Monastry are the mawles - two in number, of stone
- which are said to have contained the Holy Water.
They are quite perfect.

"I ascended the ruins of the Tower: their
appearance looked awful, they seemed every moment
ready to fall. I descended with less reluctance for
I was no sooner up than I was down again.
Historians inform you that part of the Holy Cross
was here deposited from whence it derived its name,
the Abby Vally Cruces being erected in a Vally. The
scenery about is extreemly noble and grand."

***

The "Abby" no longer looks awful and ready to fall,
but carefully preserved and neatly grassed. The
walls and arches and great windows are still
majestic, in spite of Henry 8th. Having held its
dignity and grace through seven centuries of
weather, warfare and royal vandalism, it is
pitiful that the 20th Century should have dumped
a sprawling caravan site at its gate.

(59)

Valle Crucis Abbey

Llantysilio Church

Storm Photography

26

Chain Bridge - Valle Crucis
1.8 miles   3 kms

A splendid short route, passing the Horseshoe Falls, and climbing the steep hill known as Coed Hyrddyn. Here you have views of all the surrounding hills, Dinas Bran and the Abbey.

Llantysilio Church is dedicated to St Tysilio, an early Bishop of St Asaph. Some of the present building dates from the 15th century with later embellishments.

Chain Bridge to Valle Crucis

(1) From canal by CB Hotel, go UPSTREAM on canal to its end.

(2) Follow field path to church & lane. Go R to junction with road R & lane L.

(3) Take lane L, pass 2 tracks & house L to R bend.

(4) Count 55 paces & go R on small path to telegraph pole. Go L to next pole & take stile.

(5) Climb to crest & follow ridge. Keep L til from dip you have HEAD ON view of Abbey door.   There is small TV mast just ahead.

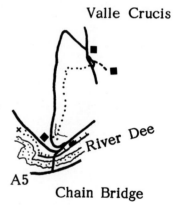

Valle Crucis

River Dee

A5

Chain Bridge

(6) Go down R to stile & A542, & L a few yards to   Abbey entrance.

Valle Crucis
●

>> OPTIONS <<
Routes 25(a) & 24(1)

＊

Valle Crucis to Chain Bridge

(a) At Abbey entrance on A542, put your back to Abbey & go L to end of slip road. Cross road & take stile.

(b) Go straight up to crest, then L along ridge, keep on R, to small TV mast R.

(c) Go on to last peak, bearing L to find path round steep bit.

(d) Sight power pole below & telegraph pole by stile. Make for stile.

(e) Go ahead to next pole, then R to lane. Go L & round bend to road.

(f) Go R to church. Take path L beside it. Follow field path past falls to canal.

(g) Take towpath to

Chain Bridge.

●

>> OPTIONS <<

Routes 27(1) & (A)

Some 400 yards from the entrance to the Abbey is the Eliseg Pillar, and this is what Mr Steele thought about it.

"From these ruins we crossed two fields in the vally for the purpose of viewing an antient Pillar - in our Road we passed a Flannel Mill [now only foundations remain in the garden of Pandy, a private house]. This Pillar is said to have been created 1500 years ago [actually, by Cyngen d854 AD, in memory of his grandfather Elise who "annexed the land of Powys by fire and sword"] and remained for ages upon the ground [after being vandalised by the Parliamentarian Army in the Civil War] till one "T Lloyd de Trevor hall" reerected it in AD 1779."

27

Chain Bridge - Barber's Hill
3.25 miles   5.25 kms

A walk along quiet lanes and a forest track in a
remote and hilly landscape. There is a level
section near the Dee, a steep track through the
timber and wide views from near Barber's Hill.

Berwyn Station was on the Corwen - Llangollen
Railway which opened for passengers in 1865.
Absorbed by the Great Western Railway in 1896 it
was closed in Dr Beeching's butchery of British
railways in 1965. The track was removed but later
relaid by the Llangollen Railway Society. At
present steam trains run from Llangollen to
Deeside Halt, but they plan to open it to
Glydyfyrdwy soon and eventually to Corwen.

Barber's Hill (Moel Geraint) is named after the
legendary barber who was gibbeted on its summit. A
barber's pole marked the spot for many years, and
was seen by George Borrow in 1854. An old lady
from whom he bought a glass of milk said that the
barber had murdered his wife "many years ago".

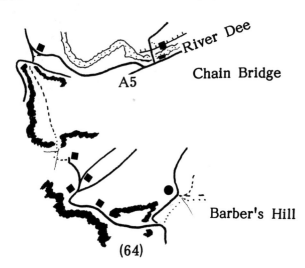

(64)

Chain Bridge
to Barber's Hill

(1) From canal, take steel footbridge near hotel canopy & follow steps to road. Go L over Dee to A5

(2) Go R & take 1st lane R. Follow appx .7 mile & round L bend to farm. Take track L to lane & go L to A5.

(3) Cross & take forest track (becomes path) appx .6 mile. As it peters out meet iron fence on L.

(4) Go R along iron fence on your L to corner & cross sheep fence. Keep same line, down valley & up, to take stile L.

(5) Follow green track, pass farm L to join stone track & on to lane junction.

(6) Go R to bridge & then R appx .7 mile to lane junction.

(7) Go L to sharp L bend where 2 tracks lead off.

(Track L leads to summit & radio mast.)

Barber's Hill
●
>> OPTIONS <<
Routes 1(a) & 2(1)

Barber's Hill to Chain Bridge

(a) At bend of lane with 2 tracks off, put your back to tracks & take lane L to junction. Go R appx .7 mile to junction bridge.

(b) Cross bridge & go appx 300 yds to wall postbox. Take track L, pass farm R & via green track to take stile.

(c) Go R, down valley then up, to corner of wire & iron fences. Cross wire fence. Go up with iron fence on your R to 3rd of diagonal braces & on appx 6 paces.

(d) Bear L to find path & follow (becomes track) appx .6 mile to A5.

(e) Take lane opposite 200 yds, & track R to lane. Go ahead appx .7 mile to rejoin A5.

(f) Go L, take road bridge across Dee. NB end of stone parapet R; just past it take steps R to canal.

Chain Bridge
●
>> OPTIONS <<
Routes 26(1) & (A)

(65)

Llangollen Canal Sections

The canal from Horseshoe Falls to Trevor Basin was built as a water supply feeder to the Ellesmere Canal. This was the original name for the waterway from Trevor past Ellesmere to Hurleston Junction, and north via Chester to Ellesmere Port and the Mersey. Later the section from Hurleston to Ellesmere Port became known as the Shropshire Union Main Line, and the section from Hurleston to the Horseshoe Falls as the Llangollen Canal.

The feeder was not intended for navigation beyond Trevor but could be used by half laden boats. It is now used by pleasure craft, the larger ones have some difficulty. The Horseshoe Falls is a magnificent semi circular weir in the River Dee, built solely for the canal by Telford in 1808. Its purpose was commercial and practical, but the great engineering structures of the time were usually beautiful. The valve house was built in 1947 to control the flow of water.

The directions refer to UPSTREAM and DOWNSTREAM on the canal, you can easily see the flow.

Irish Bridge - see Route 11

(66)

(A) UPSTREAM
Motor Museum to Chain Bridge

From Motor Museum go UPSTREAM appx .6 mile to Chain Bridge Hotel.

(B) UPSTREAM
Llangollen to Motor Museum

[From Tourist Information Office, cross Dee & go R to end of hotel, then L to canal.]

From cafe by bridge go UPSTREAM appx 1.3 miles to Motor Museum (name on green water tank L).

(C) UPSTREAM
Sun Trevor to Llangollen

From Sun Inn cross road to join towpath. Go UPSTREAM appx 1.8 miles to cafe by bridge.

(D) UPSTREAM
Bryn Howel to Sun Trevor

From B H Hotel join towpath & go UPSTREAM appx 1.6 miles to 3rd bridge. Sun Inn is across road on R.

(E) UPSTREAM
Trevor Basin to Bryn Howel

Leave canal basin via steps to road on inner end. Pass Telford pub to junction. Go L & join canal towpath R.

Go UPSTREAM appx 1.6 miles to 3rd STONE bridge (ignore small steel ones). B H Hotel is on R.

(F) UPSTREAM
Froncysyllte to Trevor Basin

[From Aqueduct Inn face it & go R appx 75 yds. Turn L & take road R down to canal & lift bridge.]

From lift bridge go UPSTREAM & cross aqueduct to Canal Basin.

(G) UPSTREAM
Irish Bridge to Froncysyllte

From road bridge go UPSTREAM appx 1 mile to lift bridge.

[For Aqueduct Inn, cross & go L uphill.]

(H) UPSTREAM
Chirk to Irish Bridge

From Chirk Station car park, cross railway & go R down to canal. Go UPSTREAM appx 2.6 miles, thro tunnel, & on to 2nd bridge.

Down

(A) DOWNSTREAM
Chain Bridge to Motor Museum

From Chain Bridge Hotel go DOWNSTREAM appx .6 mile to Motor Museum (name on green water tank R).

(B) DOWNSTREAM
Motor Museum to Llangollen

From Motor Museum go DOWNSTREAM appx 1.3 miles to 3rd bridge with cafe R.

(C) DOWNSTREAM
Llangollen to Sun Trevor

[From Tourist Information Office, cross Dee & go R to end of hotel, then L to canal.]

From cafe by bridge go DOWNSTREAM appx 1.8 miles to 3rd bridge. Sun Inn is across road on L.

(D) DOWNSTREAM
Sun Trevor to Bryn Howel

From Sun Inn get onto towpath & go DOWNSTREAM appx .6 mile to 3rd bridge. Bryn Howel Hotel is on L.

(E) DOWNSTREAM
Bryn Howel to Trevor Basin

From B H Hotel go DOWNSTREAM appx 1.6 miles to end of towpath. Go L to road junction & R past pub to enter canal basin.

(F) DOWNSTREAM
Trevor Basin to Froncysyllte

From canal basin cross aqueduct & go on to lifting bridge (.6 miles appx). [For Aqueduct Inn cross & go up L.]

(G) DOWNSTREAM
Froncysyllte to Irish Bridge

[From Aqueduct Inn, face it & go R appx 75 yds. Turn L & take road R down to canal & lift bridge.]

From lift bridge go DOWNSTREAM appx 1 mile to first bridge.

(H) DOWNSTREAM
Irish Bridge to Chirk

From road bridge over canal, go DOWNSTREAM appx 2.6 miles to Chirk Castle sign L & tunnel mouth. Go up bank to lane & L to station.

Mr Steele departs .....

"From Plas naywdd my Friend + I returned to the
Inn where we gave orders for the Chaise to be got
ready + everything requisited to be done
preparatory to the departure of two such August
Personages as I and my friend. In the interval of
time which elapsed prior to our departure we amused
ourselves by inspecting the Wellington Room, a room
well known to the frequenters of this house. Upon
the entrance to your right is a Print of his
Majesty + on the left is likewise one of Wellington
facing us as we entered.

"Llangothlin is a Place of very little Note but
most delightfully situated. It is a noted place for
Eels which are procured in great abundance. Poultry
likewise is in great abundance and very reasonable.
The distance 192 Miles from London - contains 289
houses and 1287 inhabitants.

"Left the place to return to Wrexham, past 7
o'clock Even'g, by the Hollyhead road. The Sun had
just set below the Western Hemisphere + the
feathered Tribe returned to rest when Creation
clad in Nightly Gloom presented a Scene which
call'd forth renewed fresh Contemplation on the
wonderful work of the Deity.

"About 3 miles from Llangollen we passed a Public
House on the right called the Rockman's Arms [after
the lime quarry workers at Froncysyllte], about two
miles from which we leave the Hollyhead Road and
the aqueduct a short distance to the left."

****

(69)

Berwyn Station – nostalgia at last